I CAN SHARE

MARLA CONN

Photo Glossary

 **bike**

 **book**

 **chair**

 crayons

 music

 snack

High Frequency Words:
- can
- I
- my
- share

I can share my **chair**.

crayons

I can share my **crayons**.

I can share my **bike**.

I can share my **music**.

I can share my **snack**.

I can share my **book**.

Activity

1. Go back to the story with a reading partner. Discuss how the children share.

2. As a class, discuss how sharing can be difficult
   - when something is new.
   - when something was given by a special person.
   - when something is fragile.
   - when you do not have a lot of something.

3. Brainstorm ways to problem-solve in these situations.

4. On a separate sheet of paper, write a sentence and draw a picture.

   I like to share my _____

   with _____.